DISCERNMENT

The Value of Right Choices
and How to Make Them

Walt Brock

DISCERNMENT

IRON SHARPENETH IRON PUBLICATIONS
Newberry Springs, California

Other Books by Walt Brock

Teaching Responsibility
Teaching Obedience
Dangerous Parenting Detours
Value of Camp

Table of Contents

CHAPTER ONE

What Is Discernment?

If thou seekest … searchest for her as for hid treasures.
Proverbs 2:2–5

Have you ever done something foolish even though at the time you had a suspicion it was foolish? I did exactly that when I was twelve years old. I needed a bicycle chain off one bicycle to put on another, and I didn't know anything about master links and how to take chains apart to replace them. Instead, I took a hacksaw and cut the bicycle frame in two! I ruined a good bicycle to get the chain for an older, worn-out bike. I was ignorant, too impatient to wait, and in too much of a hurry to ask my dad about it. And boy, oh boy, did I ever pay the price for that learning experience! To make things worse, when I tried to put the chain on my bike, it didn't fit. I did all that for nothing!

In hindsight, it is easy to see that I lacked the wisdom and discernment in my decision-making process. I did things the wrong way, not knowing doing it the right way would have been much easier and effective. Unfortunately, I just didn't know what the right way was. This book teaches how to make right choices on what really matters. It shows how to be discerning and how to make the right choice between two life issues (without doing something foolish like cutting a bicycle in two).

This book is designed for born-again believers desiring to please God by making the right choices in life, but who aren't sure which options please God. All believers are inundated by many choices in life and often don't know if the Bible addresses their present issues. When trying to find the definite answer, they just can't seem to find it. How can they know if what they want to participate in is right or wrong, good or bad, acceptable or unacceptable in God's eyes?

This book's goal is to provide believers with biblical tools so they can discern between what is acceptable or unacceptable to God, and about what is right or wrong in a culture that has blurred those distinctions. If believers want to know God's will and make wise decisions, they must learn to be discerning. If they desire the rich and full life God intends for them to experience and enjoy, they must make wise decisions and choices that will result in His blessing. Ultimately, the goal is making wise, God-glorifying decisions.

Most people are aware that today's generation is facing temptations and life issues previous generations never had to face. Previous generations never had to make choices about things like internet options, video games, social media, or various entertainment options available by cable, satellite, or internet.

The Bible is silent about all these new modern choices, so how can one know what pleases God? How can one not foolishly damage something in his life far more valuable than either of the choices in front of him at that moment in time? By learning to be discerning!

WHAT IS DISCERNMENT?

One of the real keys to learning discernment is to understand what is included in the definition of this learned skill. Discernment involves the following:

- Thinking and considering with a mind aimed at understanding

- Making value judgments concerning good or evil

- Making decisions about right and wrong

- Determining to hold fast to the standard of God's truth—no matter the cost

- Knowing what the issues are

- Distinguishing between two similar issues

- Finding little differences that change meanings

- Identifying falsehood disguised with partial truth

- Applying the wisdom gained from knowledge, experience, and understanding

The Webster's 1828 dictionary[1] , which gives us the closest English defini-tions to the time when the King James Version was translated, gives the following definition for discernment:

- **DISCERNMENT**, *n. the act of discerning; also, the power or faculty of the mind, by which it distinguishes one thing from another, as truth from falsehood, virtue from vice; acuteness of judgment; power of perceiving differences of things or ideas, and their relations and tendencies.*

- **DISCERN**, *to separate or distinguish or to see the difference between two or more things; to discriminate*

In this book, discernment is defined in this way:

> *The ability to see or understand the difference, to distinguish between right and wrong or good and evil. Discernment is having wisdom to apply biblical precepts and principles to a variety of situations and questions and distinguishing which way or which answer is more pleasing to God. Biblical discernment is the ability to see with the eyes of faith God's viewpoint on any given issue.*

TWO FINAL THOUGHTS ABOUT THE NATURE OF DISCERNMENT

Scripture (*Hebrews 5:14*) tells us two things about discernment. First, those with the skill and ability of discernment can find the answers to what is right and wrong, or good and evil. Second, discernment is a learned skill, and the path to learning that skill includes an understanding of Scripture, spiritual maturity, and experience in applying Scripture to daily life issues. This book shares that learning process.

> **BIBLICAL DISCERNMENT**
> is the ability to see with the eyes of faith God's
> viewpoint on any given issue.

---

1   "discernment" and "discern." *WebstersDictionary1828.com*. 2019. Web. 30 April 2019.

CHAPTER TWO

Why Is Discernment Important?

Lest Satan should get an advantage of us: for we are not ignorant of his devices. 2 Corinthians 2:11

When God created mankind, He gave man a free will—the ability to choose to obey or not obey, to please God or to please self. Satan in his opposition to God saw the creation of mankind as a way to get back at God and began an aggressive campaign of tempting Eve to violate the one command God gave to Adam and Eve. The Bible is unclear as to the specifics of the temptation, but I doubt it was a single event temptation. It probably went on for a while by planting the seeds of doubt in the mind of Eve. However, it does not appear she consulted Adam before she ate the fruit. A couple things we can learn from this, 1) Satan is relentless and does not quit as long as he perceives he has a listening ear, and 2) he seeks to isolate the one he is tempting from sources of advice and help.

TEMPTATION REPACKAGED

We already identified the forms of temptation we face today are different from those in previous years; however, these temptations can be viewed in two ways.

If we look at the specific temptations, they are different in form in our modern world, but only from the physical aspect. We may even think today's temptations are much worse than previous generations faced, but we must also see temptations from a spiritual viewpoint. When we do, a different conclusion becomes clear... in essence, they are the same. Yes, the specific life issues and temptations this generation faces are different from previous generations, but the underlying temptations involved and the sources of the temptations remain the same since Satan tempted Eve in the Garden of Eden.

From generation to generation the specific issues and questions may differ as society changes and new options of behavior are introduced into society, but the basic issues remain the same revolving around the three basic temptations Satan brought to Eve in the Garden (Genesis 3). They were presented to her in the form of questions she failed to answer with discernment. Thus she fell into Satan's trap and consequently sinned. We see these same basic temptations again when Satan tempted Jesus (*Matthew 4:1–11*) after He had fasted forty days. Satan presented the same three basic temptations, but he presented them in a different form by offering Jesus shortcuts to His desired goals—shortcuts that violated God's way and the principles of the Word of God. Jesus, using discernment, answered Satan with Scripture all three times, and thus successfully resisted temptation.

The difference in the results of these two pivotal times of temptations was not a difference in the temptations! Although they were worded differently, they were in essence the same temptation—just repackaged to fit the current situation. The difference was in the answers. Eve misquoted

God and gave her own opinions. Jesus, using wise discernment, answered Satan every time with Scripture precepts and principles.

New Testament Christians are warned in *1 John 2:15–16* to be on guard against these three basic forms of temptations. We must constantly remember Satan will always just repackage the same old temptations into new ones.

WHY CAN'T I BE LIKE EVERYONE ELSE? EVERYONE ELSE IS DOING IT!

Young people will often ask why there should be a difference between the way Christians live and the way society in general lives and behaves. They wonder why they cannot be like their neighbors and peers, or they wonder what is right and what is wrong. This is a natural question and needs to be honestly answered. Where will the answer come from? In order to answer, you must learn the skill of wise discernment and be able to give a true and honest answer to the questions of right or wrong.

> 1 Peter 3:15—*But sanctify the Lord God in your hearts: and be ready always to give an answer to every man that asketh you a reason of the hope that is in you with meekness and fear.*

The answer is not to eliminate temptations, for there will always be temptations until the Lord Jesus Christ judges Satan in the end times. Until then we live in a world filled with temptation. If we are going to be the next generation to stand for truth and righteousness in a sinful world and society, we must learn to be discerning so we can give an answer to the issues and questions of life with which this generation wrestles.

Because of the different forms and sources of temptations, identifying and resisting is not easy. Satan is sneaky and deceitful, and his temptations are spoken of in the Bible as "the wiles of the devil." To identify and stand against such wiles and recognize and experience all the good things God has given us to richly enjoy takes discernment (*1 Timothy 6:17b*). Discernment will recognize those good things from God as opposed to Satan's repackaged temptations with an element of truth included, making it hard to tell the difference between the right and wrong, or good and evil.

DISCERNMENT IS IMPORTANT BECAUSE ERROR IS SUBTLY PRESENTED

At the heart of discernment is the wisdom of distinguishing God's truth from subtly presented error. The need for such discernment is highlighted by the command of God to believers found in Colossians 2:6–8:

> *As ye have therefore received Christ Jesus the Lord, so walk ye in him: Rooted and built up in him, and stablished in the faith, as ye have been taught, abounding therein with thanksgiving. Beware lest any man spoil you through philosophy and vain deceit, after the tradition of men, after the rudiments of the world, and not after Christ.*

Concentrating on verse eight for now, we see a dire warning to the believers in Colosse to be on guard against anyone trying to use philosophical arguments to steal away their true faith. These arguments are identified as containing deceitful and empty ideas with their roots in man's fallible traditions and worldly way of thinking. False teachers and philosophers attacked the Colossians, as well as many of the other early churches, telling them Paul's teaching was acceptable only when combined with their previous religious thoughts or philosophies of life. Because of this meshing together of the gospel with other philosophies like "will worship" (stoicism) or "eat drink and be merry" (epicureanism), they were changing the truth of the gospel of grace into the error of a works-based religion. Paul wrote this letter to combat the new "wiles of the devil" method of attacking the truth.

DISCERNMENT IS IMPORTANT BECAUSE OF A DANGEROUS COMPROMISE

Just like he did in Colosse, the devil is using a common tactic today by mixing the elements of the gospel's truth into many false religions common in our world today. Those differences, although they are deceitful, can be identified if one has any basic biblical knowledge.

The challenge for us today, however, is not the false religions, but the dangerous compromise found in the false philosophies of life the devil uses to neutralize Christians for the cause of Christ. To illustrate how this danger is attacking believers today, look at the widely held and followed philosophy introduced by Johann Fichte, a German philosopher in the late 1700s. He devised the triadic idea "thesis–antithesis–synthesis" as a formula for the explanation of change. It started with 1) *a beginning proposition called a thesis,* 2) *a negation of that thesis called the antithesis, and* 3) *a synthesis whereby the two conflicting ideas are reconciled to form a new proposition.*

Anytime one blends truth with error, it becomes error. This is true even though that error may be logical and reasonable, and in our society not only legal, but commonly practiced and considered normal by our society. However, when truth is mixed with error, it becomes pure error. For example, it has become the accepted practice in society, in general, for young couples to live together before they marry. This is not illegal, and the earlier moral stigma in general is gone. But it is considered a sin by God for any sexual relationships to occur outside the marriage vows. In this case, the devil has sold our society a deceitful lie that this practice will help in eliminating marriages that just would not work. In reality, the practice has done much to destroy the sanctity of marriage and cohesiveness of the family through this synthesis philosophy steeped in the philosophy of relativism and situation ethics.

We will illustrate it this way:

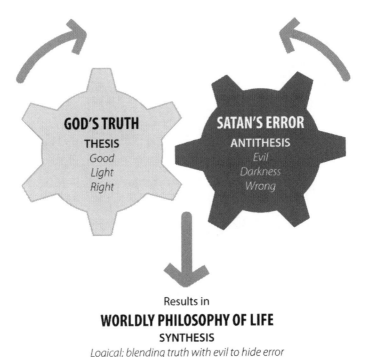

Results in
WORLDLY PHILOSOPHY OF LIFE
SYNTHESIS
Logical; blending truth with evil to hide error

DISCERNMENT IS IMPORTANT IN ORDER TO IDENTIFY SYNTHESIS

The need for discernment is not so much in separating truth from error as it is separating truth from the results of the mixture of truth and error called *synthesis*. The evil one is smart enough to be constantly repackaging his temptations in half-truth, logic, peer practice, and reasonableness as he did way back in the Garden of Eden. Compromising truth with a little error mixed into the truth is the fatal flaw of this kind of thinking—for it leads to pure error. We need to be spiritually mature men and women with the learned skill of discernment so we can choose wisely when presented with synthesis regarding the issues of life choices we face.

Remember, discernment is understanding biblical principles, thinking right, making the right judgments, and deciding right so one can do right. Discernment can and should be learned and developed, and you can do all things through Christ who strengthens you (*Philippians 4:13*).

IDEA

Instead of trying to learn all the various deceitful ways Satan may repackage his same basic temptations for effectiveness in our ever-changing contemporary culture, it is best to concentrate on learning the truth of the Word of God to use in a discerning way to identify and resist the temptations of the devil (*James 4:7*).

Sanctify them through thy truth: thy word is truth.
John 17:17

Consider Questions

Look up and discuss the temptations the devil brought to Eve and Jesus and identify how they are really the same temptation presented in different forms. Do these passages give us any ideas on how such temptations can be resisted? How might these same temptations be presented to us today in the form of our contemporary life issues?

1. *Genesis 3:1–11*—What were the three temptations aimed at Eve?

    a.

    b.

    c.

2. How did Satan change the truth into a lie?

    a.

    b.

    c.

3. *Matthew 4:1–11*—What were the three temptations aimed at Jesus?

    a.

    b.

    c.

4. How did Satan change the truth into a lie?

    a.

    b.

    c.

5. *1 John 2:15–17*—How do we fight temptations to sin originating from these three sources of temptation? Find one or more answers in each passage of Scripture.

    a. Our flesh—*Galatians 2:20; 5:16–26*

    b. The world—*1 John 5:4; Romans 12:1–2*

    c. The devil—*1 Peter 5:8–10; Ephesians 6:10–18*

    Which method of resistance to temptation is common to all three?

6. Why should a Christian live differently than everyone else? What truth or principle from each of these passages will help equip me to recognize and resist Satan's deceitful temptations?

    a. *1 John 2:17*

b. *John 17:14–18*

c. *John 13:35*

7. What weapons of spiritual warfare does Scripture provide to resist the wiles of the devil? How can they help us resist the temptations of Satan? *Ephesians 6:10–18*

a.

b.

c.

d.

e.

f.

g.

CHAPTER THREE

The Biblical Basis for Learning Discernment

The fear of the LORD is the beginning of wisdom: a good understanding have all they that do his commandments.
Psalm 111:10a

A SOLID FOUNDATION

Foundations are important. They protect a structure from shifting, lifting, or sinking. If a foundation is strong and square, the structure will be stable and true; if not, the building will be compromised at its core. When a foundation is not adequate, the building runs the risk of becoming unusable. The Lord spoke of the importance of a strong foundation in a parable in Luke's Gospel:

> Luke 6:46–49—And *why call ye me, Lord, Lord, and do not the things which I say? Whosoever cometh to me, and* **heareth my sayings, and doeth them,** *I will shew you to whom he is like: He is like a man which*

built an house, and digged deep, and laid the foundation on a rock: and when the flood arose, the stream beat vehemently upon that house, and could not shake it: for it was founded upon a rock. But **he that heareth, and doeth not**, *is like a man that without a foundation built an house upon the earth; against which the stream did beat vehemently, and immediately it fell; and the ruin of that house was great.*

In this parable the Lord made two comparisons: 1) He compares the man who knows the Word but doesn't obey it to the foolish man who built his house on sand without a foundation, and 2) He compared the wise man who knows the Word, obeys it, and lives by the Word to the man who built his house on a solid rock foundation. While the first thing new Christians should do is begin studying the Word, they must understand that just *knowing* the Word does not build a strong foundation for life. A solid foundation comes by combining a knowledge of the Word with obedience to it. Studying the Word must be accompanied with an honest decision to yield to and obey the teachings of God's Word. As you read these words from our Lord, notice the storms and floods of life came upon everyone, regardless of their life foundations. Only those with the solid rock foundation of knowing, yielding to, and obeying the Word stood strong throughout the trials and floods of life.

In learning to be discerning, you must start with a decision to grow in the knowledge of the Word of God and obey it after studying and understanding its teachings. Many years ago, my wife was talking to a young man while working together on a camp project. He said to her in all earnestness, "I just wish God would show me exactly what He wants me to do so I could decide whether to do it or not." God does not reveal His will to you so you can decide whether or not to obey it, but He reveals it to you so you will obey it! You must never forget that!

WHAT DOES THE BIBLE SAY ABOUT LEARNING DISCERNMENT?

Several Scripture passages indicate discernment development is a learned skill and comes through a learning process involving praying for wisdom, learning the Word, understanding and accepting what Scripture teaches, and listening to the teaching of the wise. This chapter shares two of those passages—one from the book of Proverbs in the Old Testament, and the other from the book of Hebrews in the New Testament.

Proverbs 1:1–7 introduces us to the author, Solomon, to whom God gave great wisdom in *1 Kings 3:9*. The primary stated purpose for the book of Proverbs is to teach the young and simple the wisdom necessary to develop discernment…but they must willingly receive it. The secondary stated purpose for writing Proverbs is to teach those already mature and wise how to grow and increase in learning and understanding—even in the more difficult areas of interpreting truth. The contrast of the first and second parts of verse seven almost takes on the flavor of a warning. Either start right with a reverential respect and trust in God (fear), or end up being a fool who chooses to go his own way. The beginning sentence of this verse is considered by many commentators to be the theme verse or motto of the book of Proverbs.

> **The fear of the Lord is the beginning of knowledge.**
> *Proverbs 1:7*

Verses	Definitions
(1) *The proverbs of Solomon the son of David, king of Israel;* (2) *To know wisdom and* **instruction***; to* **perceive** *the words of* **understanding***;* (3) **To receive** *the instruction of* **wisdom***, justice, and judgment, and equity;* (4) *To give* **subtlety** *to the* **simple***, to the young man knowledge and discretion.* (5) *A wise man will hear, and will increase learning; and a man of* **understanding** *shall attain unto wise counsels:* (6) *To understand a proverb, and the interpretation; the words of the wise, and their dark sayings.* (7) *The* **fear of the LORD** *is the beginning knowledge: but fools despise* **wisdom** *and instruction.*	**Instruction**—includes the discipline of the training process and may include chastisement, if needed **Perceive**—"to separate mentally, to distinguish;" the idea here is to understand the purpose of these writings **Understanding**—to comprehend these words and writings which will enable the willing learner to discern good and evil **Receive**—to accept the teaching, to take away and use **Subtlety**— being prudent (wise) and having discretion **Simple**—a term for one who is inexperienced (young) and easily lead to either good or evil; a novice **Discretion**—one has the wariness or wisdom to escape evil and find or choose good **Fear of the Lord**—a reverential respect and trust in God **Wisdom**—the right use of knowledge, but discernment is using wisdom to make choices and decisions that please God

Keys to Learning Discernment from Proverbs 1:1–7—the subtlety promised in verse four:

- Know the Word of God through instruction.

- Understand (perceive) the instruction.

- Receive or accept the instruction as true and good to do.

Result:

- The novice (simple) learns discretion and discernment.

- The wise will continue to learn and increase in understanding.

Hebrews 5:11–14

This passage reveals those understanding the "strong meat" of the Word are spiritually mature (of full age) and trained to "discern both good and evil." Therefore, learning discernment and gaining spiritual maturity is through studying the Word of God and using that knowledge. The recipients of this letter had not lived up to the author's expectation of growing in their spiritual lives, and were identified as needing to learn more of the Word (dull of hearing or "lazy-eared"; in other words, they were lazy in learning) and still immature in their understanding and knowledge of the Scriptures (they were able to understand the milk of Word; but not able to receive the meat of the Word; therefore, they were still as babes in Christ). The passage contains the two keys to learning discernment— *learn the Word and do it*.

Breaking this passage down verse by verse and looking again at some of the definitions helps in knowing how to develop the learned skill of discernment.

ACQUIRING BIBLICAL DISCERNMENT

Requires learning and using God's Word so one can make choices consistent with the truth of His Word.

Verses	Definitions
(11) Of whom we have many things to say, and hard to be uttered, seeing ye are dull of hearing.	**Babe** *refers to one who is spiritually immature and only able to understand the simple basics (milk) of the Word of God.*
(12) For when for the time ye ought to be teachers, ye have need that one teach you again which be the first principles of the oracles of God; and are become such as have need of **milk**, *and not of* **strong meat**.	**Strong meat and full age** *refers to one who is spiritually mature (full age) and able to understand the deeper things of the Word of God (meat).*
(13) For every one that useth **milk** *is unskilful in the word of righteousness: for he is a* **babe**.	**Exercised** *is the training and practice of the use of one's senses.*
(14) But **strong meat** *belongeth to them that are of* **full age**, *even those who* **by reason of use** *have their* **senses** *exercised to* **discern both good and evil**.	**By reason of use** *is the heart of this verse and refers to the practice and use of the Scriptures until their use is perfected and they become a habit.*
	Senses *refer to one's powers of perception and judgment.*
	Discern both good and evil *is obviously the goal of becoming a person with the learned skill of discernment.*

Keys to Learning Discernment

- Keep studying and learning Scripture until you understand it as a mature believer.

- Use Scripture constantly (exercising your learning muscle through training and practice) even as you are learning it.

```
PRACTICE MAKES PERFECT!
```

Consider Questions

1. How do you plan to learn more of God's Word?

    When—

    Where—

    How—

    Why—

2. What is your plan for using what you've learned?

3. *Proverbs 1:2–4*—List ten things a person should learn. See if you can list all ten. Now indicate which ones you need to learn the most. Group them by A, B, or C or prioritize them all by numbering them 1–10.

4. Read *Hebrews 5:11–13* and honestly evaluate your personal knowledge of the Word of God.

   a. Can you give a Bible answer if you are asked why you do or do not do something others in our society in general would do differently? (*1 Peter 3:15*)

   b. A "babe in Christ" is one who has been saved just a short while and is just starting to learn the Word of God in depth—beyond "the first principles." In the space below, record the approximate number of years you have been saved and honestly evaluate your knowledge and understanding of the Scriptures.

   • I was saved when I was _____years old, _____years ago.

   • On a scale of 1 to 10, record a comparison of where you are personally on the process continuum of moving from being a babe in Christ(1) to being a discerning, spiritually mature believer (10).

   _____   Here is where I think I am.

   _____   Here is where I should probably be by now.

5. The last life issue I personally studied the Bible diligently to determine whether it was "good or evil" was…

And my conclusion was...

Which was based on this passage of Scripture _____

6. Is your personal assessment of your need to grow in wisdom and discernment best described by either

☐ A novice (*Proverbs 1:2–4*)

☐ A wise man (*Proverbs 1:5–6*)

7. Explain why you chose one over the other and then record a specific goal for learning to be more discerning.

Why—

Goal—

CHAPTER FOUR

The Prerequisites of Learning Discernment

Only one life, 'twill soon be past; only what's done for Christ will last. –C.T. Studd

I really don't know how old I was when I came upon the fancy word *prerequisite,* but I reckon I was older than I should have been to know what it meant. I looked it up and found out it meant very simply, "required beforehand." That's a simple definition, and I was embarrassed I hadn't known it. But once I knew, it gave me no comfort, because I knew what the word *required* meant! It meant I couldn't continue until a necessary condition had been fulfilled.

If one is going to truly learn the skill of discernment concerning life issues—whether they are daily issues, life direction issues, or changing times and culture issues, the following prerequisites are a necessary condition to proceed.

PREREQUISITES IN BRIEF

1. Saved—Are you sure you are saved?

2. Faith—Is your faith what it should be?

3. Yielded—Are you willing to go God's way if it is different from your way?

4. Committed—Are you willing to pay the price to learn discernment?

    — the cost of praying earnestly for it

    — the cost of spending time in the Word and prayer for insight and understanding

    — the cost of working hard to learn

5. Desire—The passion to work on developing the ability to discern between good and evil. Is it something you really want?

When you have honestly answered yes to these questions, you are ready to proceed to the next step. But before you answer them, it is necessary to know what is involved in each question.

EXPANDING THE QUESTIONS

Question One Expanded—SAVED

Are you sure you are saved? You must have a solid assurance of your own faith and trust in the Lord before you can proceed with faith. Since faith in the Lord Jesus Christ is an essential of salvation, this must be settled once for all.

> Romans 10:9–10—*That if thou shalt confess with thy mouth the Lord Jesus, and shalt believe in thine heart that God hath raised him from*

the dead, thou shalt be saved. For with the heart man believeth unto
righteousness; and with the mouth confession is made unto salvation.

My Answer to Question One

Write out your personal salvation testimony, including when you placed
your faith in the Lord and the circumstances surrounding that time.

Question Two Expanded—FAITH

Is your faith what it should be—both saving faith and living faith? Many
people place their faith in the Lord for their eternal salvation but stumble
a bit when it comes to transferring that faith into daily living—to trust
God to determine what is important and of value in their daily lives. The
question of faith boils down to answering this next question truthfully.

My Answer to Question Two

Do you believe (*trust in, rely on, have confidence in*) the Bible is the absolute source of truth and supersedes all other ideas, thoughts, opinions,
and philosophies put forth in this world?

Circle one: YES   NO

How would you explain your confidence to someone who asked
you why?

Question Three Expanded—YIELDED

This simple question makes all the difference. Are you willing to go God's way if it is different from your way?

My Answer to Question Three

Circle one: YES   NO

Write out a prayer of commitment to God.

Read these verses and write out what you would say to others when they wonder why you live as you do. (To get the complete context of the passage, read verses 14–28.)

> Joshua 24:14–15—*Now therefore fear the Lord, and serve him in sincerity and in truth: and put away the gods which your fathers served on the other side of the flood, and in Egypt; and serve ye the Lord. And if it seem evil unto you to serve the Lord, choose you this day whom ye will serve; whether the gods which your fathers served that were on the other side of the flood, or the gods of the Amorites, in whose land ye dwell: but as for me and my house, we will serve the Lord.*

I live as I do because …

Question Four Expanded—COMMITTED

Are you willing and committed to pay the price to learn discernment? Are you now promising to prayerfully and honestly seek to understand God's Word with a goal of knowing God's way? You will undoubtedly have a demand upon your time and effort as you undertake this endeavor. Are you committed to being diligent to learn to be discerning?

> James 1:5–6—*If any of you lack wisdom, let him ask of God, that giveth to all men liberally, and upbraideth not; and it shall be given him. But let him ask in faith, nothing wavering. For he that wavereth is like a wave of the sea driven with the wind and tossed.*

> Hebrews 11:6—*But without faith it is impossible to please him: for he that cometh to God must believe that he is, and that he is a rewarder of them that diligently seek him.*

My Answer to Question Four

I promise the Lord I will diligently pray for His wisdom and discernment.

Circle one: YES   NO

Write out a brief outline of your prayer for God's help and wisdom.

What is your plan for time spent in prayer? When, where, and how do you plan to pray?

When—

Where—

How—

Have you counted the cost to learn this skill of discernment? Read *Luke 14:25–33* as you answer this.

Circle one: YES   NO

Question Five Expanded—DESIRE

Do you really desire discernment in general, and in any particular area you are questioning? It is important to be completely honest in this quest for God's truth and ways. You should not go into this exercise with a predetermined idea of what the answer is, or should be, based on your own desires. This is a heart issue for you.

My Answer to Question Five

Read the following verses before you answer. This will take a little time, thought, and effort. Do the work.

> Psalm 51:6—*Behold, thou desirest truth in the inward parts* [one's heart]: *and in the hidden part thou shalt make me to know wisdom.* [Notice the connection of truth to wisdom given by God.]

> Jeremiah 42:20–21—*For ye dissembled in your hearts, when ye sent me unto the LORD your God, saying, Pray for us unto the LORD our God;*

and according unto all that the LORD our God shall say, so declare unto us, and we will do it. And now I have this day declared it to you; but ye have not obeyed the voice of the LORD your God, nor any thing for the which he hath sent me unto you.

Dissemble—*to deceive, go astray, wander away.* It means these people told God they would obey Him, but when the command came they did not like, they went back on their word to obey what He said.

Read the following passages as you answer. These two passages of Scripture were written to Timothy by the Apostle Paul, giving him instruction on how to grow in his spiritual life through diligent study of God's Word.

- *1 Timothy 4:15–16*

- *2 Timothy 3:14–17*

Are you willing to do the same? Record your thoughts and concerns and plans.

CHAPTER FIVE

A Recipe for Making Right Choices

All scripture is given by inspiration of God, and is profitable for doctrine, for reproof, for correction, for instruction in righteousness: that the man of God may be perfect, thoroughly furnished unto all good works.
2 Timothy 3:16–17

Learning the discernment process is like following a tried and true recipe for a delicious meal or dessert. If you follow the recipe, you usually end up with the same result over and over, but if you deviate from the recipe, the taste is just not right. The old quote, "there is no product without the process," indicates if you desire a particular result, you must follow the prescribed process. Many times you desire the end result, but you hesitate in committing to the process. You look for shortcuts but do not find any. You change the recipe, and the results are altered as well.

A good recipe usually has three parts: 1) a list of ingredients along with the amounts to be added, 2) the preparation process and related instructions, and 3) the cooking or baking instructions.

RECIPE FOR SPIRITUAL DISCERNMENT

Add the following **INGREDIENTS**:

- Prayer
- God's Word, a time of both devotion and study
- Obedience, yielding to God's revealed Word
- Advice, teaching, and counsel

PREPARATION PROCESS

Study with a prepared heart (*Ezra 7:10*), seeking the law of the Lord, both the direct precepts and the derived principles (next chapter). Then DO IT. As you begin, develop principles to live by and apply to life's issues. This will take self-discipline to mix the Word into your life with diligence and endurance.

LET IT COOK

TIME: *Endure through life's race (Hebrews 12:1–2). Spend the necessary time.*

TEMPERATURE: *Deal with the challenges of life as you grow (Job 23:10–12).*

INGREDIENTS

Prayer

Pray consistently for wisdom and understanding concerning developing discernment. Prayer is one of the prerequisites, but this is not just prayer as one starts the process. This is the "praying without ceasing," asking God for wisdom every day of your life.

> James 1:5–8—*If any of you lack wisdom, let him ask of God, that giveth to all men liberally, and upbraideth not; and it shall be given him. But let him ask in faith, nothing wavering. For he that wavereth is like a wave of the sea driven with the wind and tossed. For let not that man think that he shall receive any thing of the Lord. A double minded man is unstable in all his ways.*

These verses give reasons to pray for wisdom as well as how to pray for wisdom. Ask God for wisdom because He will not "upbraid" or scold you for your current lack if you are now seeking it. Ask God for wisdom because He answers this prayer "liberally," or *bountifully*. Ask God for wisdom without wavering (doubting God) because He answers the prayer of faith. It pleases God when you pray in faith (*Hebrews 11:6*).

This kind of prayer will involve not only personal consistency, but also asking others to pray for your ability to use His wisdom in making daily judgments and decisions. Ask others to pray for you as Paul prayed for the Philippians.

> Philippians 1:9–10—*And this I pray, that your love may abound yet more and more in knowledge and in all judgment; that ye may approve things that are excellent; that ye may be sincere and without offense till the day of Christ.*

God's Word
God's Word is the main ingredient, and leaving out or slighting His Word will absolutely ruin the final product.

Start with a time of devotion every day—a time to prepare your heart to receive His Word as you read and study it. Job used the everyday necessity of food to communicate the importance of being in the Word each day. Joshua emphasized consistency in meditation of the Word and obedience to the Word by referring to it as something he did "day and night."

> Job 23:12—*Neither have I gone back from the commandment of his lips; I have esteemed the words of his mouth more than my necessary* **food**.

> Joshua 1:8— *This book of the law shall not depart out of thy mouth; but thou shalt meditate therein* **day and night**, *that thou mayest observe to do according to all that is written therein: for then thou shalt make thy way prosperous, and then thou shalt have good success.*

It helps to keep a daily written record or journal of your blessings and challenges as you read the Word for daily devotions. Periodically review your notes and journal entries to find encouragement and inspiration for your daily living for God.

Obedience

Obedience, by yielding to what you learn in the Word, is a key ingredient. It not only makes the Word of God "sweeter than honey" to the taste, but is also beneficial to anyone partaking of this delicious meal (*Psalm 19:7–11*). Deciding ahead of time to obey the Word as you learn what it says is helpful in keeping a yielded attitude to the Scriptures. That attitude of future surrender says, "I might not know all God wants of me today, but as I study His Word and become convinced of its truth and what God desires of me, I will yield to that truth. I will be a doer of the Word."

> James 1:22—*But be ye doers of the word, and not hearers only, deceiving your own selves.*

Seek Advice

Seek advice, counsel, and input from discerning church leaders who have their "senses exercised to discern both good and evil" (*Hebrews 5:14*). Asking for help and input involves two hard-to-find ingredients: 1) the humility to ask a question about something you do not know, and 2) the faith to know God has given the church godly leaders who desire to use their developed discernment to help others grow in grace and knowledge of His Word. It is why they are in the ministry—use them!

THE PREPARATION PROCESS

Study Scripture (*Acts 20:28–32; Hebrews 4:12; 2 Timothy 2:15–16*)
This is a more in-depth study of the Word of God than one typically does in his daily devotions. Bible study concentrates on understanding what the Word *means*. Without a proper interpretation of the Word, one might

come up with all kinds of false ideas. Remember the golden rule of Bible interpretation—"context, context, context!" Begin by looking first for direct precepts and absolute commands from God. These are the direct commands of God to do or not to do something. They are clear, and God expects you to obey them without rationalizing why it might be all right to go against His clearly revealed truth.

Follow this by learning to develop principles for spiritual discernment. These are derived from a study of the Word, and they help you to think biblically through applying scriptural principles of the Word of God to your daily life. This is the real work of learning discernment. Remember the phrase from *Hebrews 5:14*, "by reason of use have their senses exercised to discern both good and evil." This is the application of that phrase—the grunt work of learning discernment. Practice over and over again the process of thinking and developing Bible principles to apply when making decisions and determining whether something is good or evil. There are no shortcuts in this process.

Keep on Growing and Learning (*1 Peter 2:2; 2 Peter 3:18; Luke 2:52*)
Scripture is clear. Christians are commanded to keep learning more of God's Word and way. Everyone starts their Christian lives as babes in Christ (understanding and belief in the essence of the gospel). It is our responsibility to learn, grow, and mature in Him until we are thoroughly prepared as people of God to do the good works He has for us to do.

> 2 Timothy 3:15–17—*And that from a child thou hast known the holy scriptures, which are able to make thee wise unto salvation through faith which is in Christ Jesus. All scripture is given by inspiration of God, and is profitable for doctrine, for reproof, for correction, for instruction in righteousness: That the man of God may be perfect, thoroughly furnished unto all good works.*

Do not be surprised that all of life's growth and learning is a process … it always has been. Seeds are planted, germinate, grow, mature, and finally yield fruit; it is always a process. Do not be surprised the process takes time and effort. Just make sure you constantly progress as you grow. Even Jesus when upon this earth had to go through this process in His spiritual and physical development before he began His earthly ministry (*Luke 2:52*).

LET IT COOK

Cooking is essential for most recipes to work. The cake needs to be in the oven for the right amount of time at the right temperature for it to bake satisfactorily. In like manner, the preparation for the skill of discernment also needs both time and temperature to bake satisfactorily. Spiritual growth from being a babe in Christ to being a spiritually mature person takes time. Do not expect it to happen overnight. It takes time for the Word of God to simmer down into your soul for daily living discernment skills. A little bit of extra heat actually helps speed up the process as you deal with the stresses and trials of life. You are challenged to dig deeper into the Word for help, to spend more time in prayer, and to seek others for advice and prayer. These all help the process, and endurance through them is necessary for the satisfactory end product.

Scripture relates this process to a race being run—a course laid out by Jesus, filled with temptations of besetting sin and extra weight you have added to your life. You are admonished to endure (with patience) to the end of the race, knowing by faith Jesus designed this life course, and He is your example, as well as your helper. He finished His race, and with His help you can finish your race. If you endure the cooking process to the end, crowns of joy await you as you learn the skill of discernment.

> Hebrews 12:1–2—*Wherefore seeing we also are compassed about with so great a cloud of witnesses, let us lay aside every weight, and the sin which doth so easily beset us, and let us run with patience the race that is set before us, looking unto Jesus the author and finisher of our*

faith; who for the joy that was set before him endured the cross, despising the shame, and is set down at the right hand of the throne of God.

> **It is good for me that I have been afflicted;**
> **that I might learn thy statues.**
> *Psalm 119:71*

Consider Questions

1. After reading more about prayer in this chapter, review your answers concerning prayer recorded in chapter four, and see if they need amending in any way.

    a. Do your plans for prayer for wisdom need any additions?

    b. Do you need to involve others through shared prayer requests?

    c. What are you asking God for that will help you with discernment?

2. Is there anything in your life you know for sure God wants you to yield to Him and obey?

3. How might you immediately put into practice the phrase "by reason of use" from *Hebrews 5:14* in your quest to develop discernment?

4. What aspect of learning discernment might take some time and determination to endure with patience the process of "cooking" (time and temperature) in your life?

5. As you have prepared this recipe and are letting it cook in your life, re-read *Hebrews 12:1* and answer the following two questions:

   a. Are there any sinful habits in your life you need to lay aside through confession, forgiveness, and change?

   b. What weights in your life keep you from being what you could be for the Lord? Will you lay them aside, too?

   c. How do the problems and challenges you face in life help you learn discernment?

CHAPTER SIX

Praying for Discernment

*For this cause we also, since the day we heard it, do not cease
to pray for you, and to desire that ye might be filled with the
knowledge of his will in all wisdom and spiritual understanding.*
Colossians 1:9

This is the third time you have come to the discussion of prayer for discernment. Too much emphasis cannot be placed on this aspect of becoming a wise, discerning person. God commands you to pray in faith without wavering, believing He answers prayer. Prayer is simply fellowshipping with God—praising Him, thanking Him with genuine gratitude, sharing your concerns and needs with Him, and asking for His forgiveness and guidance.

Chapter four looked at God's instructing believers to ask Him in faith for wisdom (*James 1*). It also showed the importance of expressing your requests to others, asking them to pray for your spiritual understanding and wisdom, as well as for health, safety, and material needs. The Apostle Paul left a good example of this service for others through prayer as he prayed for the Colossians by asking God they "might be filled with the knowledge of his will in all wisdom and spiritual understanding."

God expects you to be praying for discernment. If you indeed desire to discern God's will and ways from all other choices being constantly directed at you in our culture, your prayers for discernment must grow. This chapter considers two additional passages of Scripture: 1) *1 Kings 3:3–15* where King Solomon, when faced with the new and daunting challenge ahead of him as king, asked God for the wisdom to lead the nation, and 2) *Nehemiah 1:1–11* where two examples of prayer are given to be considered when praying for discernment .

THE PRAYER WHEN FACED WITH A LIFE CHANGE

Solomon was suddenly handed the kingship when his father David passed away. As the reality of the situation became clear to him, he realized life would never be the same again, and the responsibility before him was daunting and challenging. When God asked him what he wanted, instead of the material things of life, he asked for wisdom to make good decisions in fulfilling his responsibility as king. The request pleased the Lord, and He gave him both the wisdom and the material blessings.

Young adults today might realize things are about to change for them. Maybe they are moving out of their parents' home, starting a new college or major, considering marriage, or are married and having their first child. But whatever it is, life is changing. In times of change, it is important and necessary to ask God for the wisdom to make discerning choices. If people know change is coming for themselves, family, or friends, now is a good time to begin praying for that needed discernment in the coming decisions.

THE LONG SEASON OF PRAYER

When Nehemiah heard about the challenges and opportunity to serve the Lord through helping with the restoration process back in Jerusalem, he began to pray for the Lord's will. The huge move would require a change in job, lifestyle, location, and responsibilities. His whole life would be uprooted, but the need had gripped his heart and brought him to tears, fasting, studying the Word, and much prayer.

He began praying, and although he had continuing responsibilities in his current life and job, every spare moment for over four months he spent in the Word, in prayer, and considering what God wanted him to do about the burden He had laid on his heart. He was not just asking the same question over and over, "What should I do?" The prayers were mixed with a study of the Word and an application of Scripture to the contemporary situation he faced.

Seasons of prayer are not only long and heartfelt but also guided by consistent and in-depth Bible study so you can apply the Word to the dilemma you face, which is in essence, discernment.

An aspect of prayer not often practiced today and not commanded (though commended) in the Word, is fasting. Scripture gives examples of many men of God and the example of Jesus. In principle, fasting is voluntarily giving up something in one's discretionary time schedule for the purpose of spending that time in prayer. It could be giving up a meal, or some other form of going without, for a time of prayer. It could be a food fast, a media fast, or a recreation fast. It can be as short as one meal, or as long as several weeks, depending on the type of fast.

THE SHORT SENTENCE PRAYER

The short sentence prayer comes when you are faced with an immediate decision or action. You have no time for days of prayer. The decision or action is now, and you call out for God to help you NOW. Nehemiah did that in verse eleven of the first chapter. In the spur of the moment, a need arose for him to share with the king the burden God had laid on his heart. He prayed for the right words, the right demeanor, the right attitude, and for the king to have the right response. Notice a couple of things to remember about sentence prayers:

- They are truly sentence prayers—short and to the point. "God, give me the right words to say," or "Lord, I need your wisdom right now to make the right decision."

- To be effective, they should be preceded by seasons of prayer for wisdom and understanding of the Word, expressing a yielding to God's will and way.

The subject of sentence prayers varies greatly, but they all boil down to recognizing *right now* you need God's help, and you are willing to ask for it by following the scriptural admonition found in Hebrews 4:16:

> *Let us therefore come boldly unto the throne of grace, that we may obtain mercy, and find grace to help in time of need.*

ASKING FOR HELP

In the end, you need God's help for everything you do—even to pray correctly. The Holy Spirit comes to your aid in praying for discernment. Scriptures show the Holy Spirit's help in your prayers in two areas:

- In asking God through His Spirit to open your understanding of the Scriptures by giving you the insight to use that understanding to identify truth, increase in wisdom, and gain discernment (*1 Corinthians 2:6–16; John 16:7–14*).

John 16:13— *Howbeit when he, the Spirit of truth, is come, he will guide you into all truth: for he shall not speak of himself; but whatsoever he shall hear, that shall he speak: and he will show you things to come.*

- In asking the Holy Spirit as He intercedes for you to reveal God's will to you.

Romans 8:26-27—*Likewise the Spirit also helpeth our infirmities: for we know not what we should pray for as we ought: but the Spirit itself maketh intercession for us with groanings which cannot be uttered. And he that searcheth the hearts knoweth what is the mind of the Spirit, because he maketh intercession for the saints according to the will of God.*

THE MANNER OF YOUR PRAYER

Does the way you pray matter? Yes, it does matter! The Lord in *Matthew 6* gave instructions to the disciples concerning the way they should be praying. In verse nine He said, "After this manner therefore, pray ye …." The Lord was simply saying to the disciples, "This is the way you should pray," and He then gave them a model prayer to emulate. While the Lord's model prayer gives a good outline for the basic content of your prayers, another passage in James addresses other aspects of the manner of your prayers.

First Manner of Prayer—*Praying in faith*

James 1:5–6a—*If any of you lack wisdom, let him ask of God, that giveth to all men liberally, and upbraideth not; and it shall be given him…but let him ask in faith, nothing wavering.*

Faith is believing what the Bible says about God is true, and based upon that belief, you take action. When you pray in faith, you believe God is able, He loves you, He hears your prayers, and He will answer your prayers based upon His goodness and love. Pray the prayer of faith without doubting God's power or His goodness.

Second Manner of Prayer—*Praying energetically*

James 5:16b—*The effectual fervent prayer of a righteous man availeth much.*

When applying this verse to your prayer life, consider the definitions of the key phrase. Dictionary.com defines *fervent* as "having or showing great warmth or intensity of spirit, feeling, enthusiasm."[1] Scripture states the emotional manner in which you pray does matter to God. Your manner of praying should show the intensity of your emotions and longings for the discernment and wisdom you are asking. The emotional energy you bring to your prayers should demonstrate your strong desire for His wisdom and discernment, not just a "dry as bones" intellectual exercise. *Strong's Dictionary* also states the phrase "effectual fervent" comes from the Greek word *en-erg-eh'-o*, indicating your prayers should be "energetic" in manner.[2]

Therefore, when praying for discernment, your manner of prayer should carry an energy communicating a true inner intensity and fervency as you pray in faith—faith believing your good and loving God will both hear and answer your prayers according to His will and knowledge.

> *But without faith it is impossible to please him: for he that cometh to God must believe that he is, and that he is a rewarder of them that diligently seek him.* Hebrews 11:6

---

1   "fervent." *Dictionary.com.* 2019. Web. 30 April 2019.

2   *Strong's Exhaustive Concordance*: King James Version. Updated ed. La Habra: Lockman Foundation, 1995.

Consider Questions

1. What life-changing situations are you currently facing or will face soon? Are you now or will you in the future take these to the Lord in prayer?

2. Are you wrestling with a major issue in your life where you need to begin a season of prayer and Bible study to discern the right decision to make or direction to go in the days ahead?

3. Once you determine the issue, and your desire is to begin a season of prayer for God's help, what are your plans for this season of prayer?

   a. Time per day? How much time? _____

   b. Day of the week to spend extra time— _____

   Hours that day—_____

   c. Scripture to study concurrently?

   — Biographical study—David vs. Saul, Abraham, Jesus, Jeremiah, Paul

   — Book study—Philippians, Psalms, Proverbs

   — Word studies

d. Will you fast as part of this season of prayer? What aspects of your discretionary time will you consider setting aside for a while in order to spend that time praying? It is wise to think in terms of specifics like what, when, how much, etc.

4. When would a sentence prayer in the past have helped you with a decision or response?

5. In what situations would a sentence prayer be helpful to you in the future?

6. What are you going to ask the Holy Spirit to help you with?

7. When considering the manner of your prayers, how might you improve your prayers for discernment?

8. Look up the definition of the word *diligent* and consider whether it is a word that could also describe your manner of prayer for discernment. See *Hebrews 11:6.*

CHAPTER SEVEN

Ye Ought to Be Discerners … Already!

So then faith cometh by hearing, and hearing by the word of God.
Romans 10:17

BEING WHAT YOU OUGHT TO BE

In Scripture, *spiritual maturity* is referred to as being "complete" (*Colossians 2:10*) or "perfect" (*2 Timothy 3:17*) and is the goal of a believer's sanctification while still here on the earth (your spiritual growth from being a "babe" in Christ to becoming of "full age" in Him). As a believer, spiritual maturity should be your constant goal. Physical growth is measured in time by years, months, and days, but spiritual growth isn't measured by time but by godliness and an understanding of the Word. The question for you is, are you where you *ought* to be in your spiritual growth? Being where you ought to be is being where God wants you to be, and where you *should* be if you have been growing spiritually as a believer should.

God has given you several helpers to aid in the growth process. He has also given you a free will and expects you to use your own initiative to be pleasing to Him. God gives three other indispensable aids in your Christian walk. You will become the spiritually mature person you *ought* to be by combining all four "helpers" in your spiritual growth process, with the goal of discerning good from evil.

The Four Helpers

- Your decision and determination to grow in grace and knowledge of the Lord (*2 Peter 3:18; 2 Timothy 2:15*)

- The local church and other believers who will teach and encourage you to grow (*Ephesians 4:11–16; Hebrews 10:24–25*)

- The Holy Spirit's help to understand the Word of God (*John 16:13*), intercede in your prayers *(Romans 8:26–27)*, convict you of needed change in your life (*John 16:8*), and change you (*2 Corinthians 3:18*)

- The Word of God, your source of truth and knowledge (*2 Timothy 2:15*)

All four are gifts from God to help you make progress in your sanctification, and all are vital. This section concentrates on the Word of God's role in this process of developing discernment and begins with two Bible truths you need to understand.

1. **You are commanded by God to study the Bible.**

    2 Timothy 2:15—*Study to shew thyself approved unto God, a workman that needeth not to be ashamed, rightly dividing the word of truth.*

2. **You are to use what you learn as you live by the Word of God in this sinful world.** Others will question you, and when they do, you will have an opening to witness for the Lord.

1 Peter 3:15—*But sanctify the Lord God in your hearts: and be ready always to give an answer to every man that asketh you a reason of the hope that is in you with meekness and fear.*

Individually, how can you use the Word of God in acquiring the learned skill of discerning God's truth, will, and way from all others? The following Bible study should give you something to think about and hopefully give some instruction about how to exercise your own free will to "grow in grace, and in the knowledge of our Lord and Saviour Jesus Christ" (*2 Peter 3:18*).

Are you a babe in Christ who is unskillful in the Word, understanding only the "milk" of the Word? Or are you skillful in the Word, able to understand the "meat" of the Word and discern God's will and way? Sadly, the answer to those questions has little to do with how long you have been a Christian, but rather your use of Scripture and submission to its teaching.

Consider Questions

1. Read *Hebrews 5:11–14*—Start with prayer, read the passage, then begin filling out the chart (see page 26 for definitions).

   Hebrews 5:11–14 ... *we have many things to say, and hard to be uttered, seeing ye are dull of hearing. For when for the time ye ought to be teachers, ye have need that one teach you again which be the first principles of the oracles of God; and are become such as have need of milk, and not of strong meat. For every one that useth milk is unskilful in the word of righteousness: for he is a babe. But strong meat belongeth to them that are of full age, even those who by reason of use have their senses exercised to discern both good and evil.*

   a. What ought you to be?

   When for a _____

   You ought to be _____

   But you are _____

   b. Fill in the accompanying chart. Try to find at least ten characteristics for each side of the chart. Then check your answers on pages 109–110.

Babes in Christ	Teachers
1.	1.
2.	2.

Babes in Christ	Teachers
3.	3.
4.	4.
5.	5.
6.	6.
7.	7.
8.	8.
9.	9.
10.	10.

2. Consider the other three helpers given on page 60. Read the Bible references given and answer the questions below.

a. Have you decided to grow spiritually?

Circle one: YES   NO

If so, record your specific decision here.

b. Consider asking your pastor about the best way to request help in biblically understanding and resolving challenging issues as you have questions in your personal Bible study.

c. Is there a spiritually mature person in your church that you could ask to be your mentor and sounding board when you need advice? Establishing such a relationship in advance works best.

d. Is there anything the Holy Spirit keeps bringing to your mind? If so, what is it, and how will you use the study of the Word to address that issue?

CHAPTER EIGHT

Four Levels of Bible Study

In the beginning was the Word, and the Word was with God, and the Word was God.
John 1:1a

When you read the Bible with the goal of becoming spiritually mature, you should approach the task from four different levels of mental and spiritual focus. Try to understand what the Bible is saying (content), what it is saying to you (devotion), what it is informing you about living in this world today (study for application to life), and what is required to study for the purpose of teaching others (being able to use the Word for admonition).

FOUR LEVELS OF BIBLE STUDY

Reading for Knowledge and Content (*Proverbs 1:7, 22, 29; 2:1–9*)
It is important to just spend some time reading the Word to get a feel for the overall content and the continuity of the Scripture narratives. You

need to know what the Bible says by spending quality time in the Word and getting a good overview of its contents.

> 2 Peter 1:5—*And beside this, giving all diligence, add to your faith virtue; and ... knowledge.*

> Psalm 94:12—*Blessed is the man whom thou chastenest, O Lord, and teachest him out of thy law.*

> 2 Peter 3:18—*But grow in grace, and in the knowledge of our Lord and Saviour Jesus Christ. To him be glory both now and for ever. Amen.*

Reading for Devotion and Fellowship with God (*Psalm 25:4–12***)**
Job understood it was more important to read the Word of God than it was to spend time eating food necessary for life. He understood the spiritual was more important than the physical. Remember Jesus desires fellowship with you.

> Job 23:12b—*I have esteemed the words of his mouth more than my necessary food.*

> Revelation 3:20—*Behold, I stand at the door, and knock: if any man hear my voice, and open the door, I will come in to him, and will sup with him, and he with me.*

Study for Personal Spiritual Growth, Meditation (Application), and Obedience (*Psalm 1; 19:7–14; 119:15, 23, 48, 78, 97, 99, 148*). If you want to please the Lord and want to be discerning, spiritual growth is not an option!

> Joshua 1:8— *This book of the law shall not depart out of thy mouth; but thou shalt meditate therein day and night, that thou mayest observe to do according to all that is written therein: for then thou shalt make thy way prosperous, and then thou shalt have good success.*

This meat-of-the-Word type of studying is for personal application and decisions of life—the heart of learning discernment. This is a faith-growing process because each new unfolding of the Word challenges you to grow your faith by trusting God to love you, know what is best, and do what is good for His cause, for you, and for others. As He challenges you, He is working on you. Further chapters cover this more fully.

Study for Teaching and application to others through opportunities for decisions. You are commanded by God to be ready always to give an answer, to inform, and to teach those around you—your children, fellow church members, family, friends, and those hungry to learn (*Hebrews 5:12; 2 Timothy 2:2, 24–25; Proverbs 9:9; Deuteronomy 6:1, 7; Matthew 28:19; Acts 5:42; 1 Timothy 6:2*).

In the Old Testament, Ezra is a good example of someone who learned the Word so he could live by it and teach it to others. The following chart illustrates how this cycle can go on from generation to generation—as long as each generation gets to the teaching stage of the cycle. If one generation fails to teach the next, the cycle is interrupted, and the next generation may grow up without the knowledge of Christ—a shame to those who know Christ.

> 1 Corinthians 15:34—*Awake to righteousness, and sin not; for some have not the knowledge of God: I speak this to your shame.*

THE GENERATIONAL CYCLE

> Ezra 7:10—*For Ezra had prepared his heart to seek the law of the LORD, and to do it, and to teach in Israel statutes and judgments.*

Notice: 1) Ezra prepared his heart (yielding to and receiving the teaching of the Word), 2) then he studied the Word in-depth for the purpose of knowing the truth, so he could 3) obey it personally and consistently. His obedience validated his teaching 4) so others who heard his teaching would follow it. They, having been taught, could now choose to keep the cycle going by preparing their hearts to receive the Word, obey it, and teach it to their generation … and so on, from generation to generation. God's plan is to pass on His truth year after year until He returns.

THE GENERATIONAL CYCLE

❶

EZRA PREPARED
HIS HEART
Ezra 7:10

❹

AND TO TEACH

PREPARED   **HEART**
In view   *Mind*
of the future, *Emotion*
I set things   *Will*
in order.

❷

TO SEEK THE LAW
OF THE LORD

ETERNAL VIEW OF LIFE

*My desire and goal in life
is to please God.*

❸

AND TO DO IT

Consider Questions

1. Which of the four levels of Bible study is your

   Strength?

   Weakness?

2. How can you improve each of them?

   a.

   b.

   c.

   d.

Helpful Hints for Bible Study for Both Devotion and Personal Spiritual Growth ... Becoming Skillful as You Read God's Word

You might want to incorporate some of the following ideas into your devotional journal.

Devotional Helps

1. Use the commonly suggested questions as you do your daily devotions. A journal helps to record your answers and thoughts for later review.

   a. Is there a sin I should forsake?

   b. Is there a promise to claim?

c. Is there an example in this passage I should heed (good or bad)?

d. Is there a command to obey?

e. Is there a general principle I can apply to my life today?

f. Is there a warning for me or others to avoid?

g. Is there an others-first principle I can implement?

h. Is there something in this passage I can learn about God?

   — About His power and ability?

   — About His character?

   — About His heart and care for me?

2. What in this passage can help, improve, or hinder (if violated) my various relationships?

a. With God

b. With others

Bible Study for Personal Spiritual Growth and Application Principles
As you write out your Bible Principles...

1. Think in terms of not only action principles, but attitude principles as well.

a. Action—what I should do or how I should act

b. Attitude—how I should think, or how I should feel about it

2. Make your principles personal. Use *I, me, my,* and *mine,* and not *we, us, our,* or *yours.*

3. Be as specific as possible—not "just to be a better Christian" or "to be more like Christ." Example: I will become more Christlike by being patient when my brother...

4. Add the characteristics of good goals to your applications, such as a time element (target dates, length of time spent) and measurable goals (specific amount—read one Proverb every day before I go to bed or eat breakfast).

5. Select issues you are facing now to look for principles of application as you read or study the Word.

6. Think about some future needs of high interest—dating, courtship, marriage, God's will for college, occupation, summer service, church to join, or place to live. Look for narratives or principles addressing these issues to help you discern God's will.

7. Journal what you learn, your decisions, your progress, and especially any unresolved issues you are wrestling with, so you can revisit them as you grow in grace and knowledge of the Lord.

8. Use action verbs in your writing of principles and decisions (act, do, control, add, compose, lead, make, mark, undo, skip, start, schedule, seize, turn, write).

Additional Thoughts

1. If you are serious in your Bible study, it is important to obtain some study aids and tools.

    a. Use a Bible study program such as e-Sword (https://www.e-sword.net/) which offers its basic level free.

    b. Books also help, and some prefer them.

        — Concordance

        — Topical Bible

        — Times and customs helps

        — One-volume commentary

        — Interpretation helps (*Bible Explorer's Guide* by John Phillips is probably most helpful in learning proper interpretation skills in a format both understanding, yet challenging.)

2. Be honest with what the Scripture actually says. No more, no less. Do not add to or subtract from.

CHAPTER NINE

Developing Bible Principles for the Issues of Life

Rightly dividing the Word of Truth

In-depth Bible study is more than just reading a passage over several times or writing out what you think it means. Such Bible study takes time and effort, and this book shares one way a believer might go about such a study. It is important to know how to differentiate between Bible commands and Bible principles.

What is the difference between a Bible command (sometimes called direct precepts) and Bible principles (sometimes called derived principles)? Do they carry the same weight of authority? Why are they both necessary for learning the skill of discernment? How can you study the Bible properly to find the answers to these questions?

> 2 Timothy 2:15—*Study to shew thyself approved unto God, a workman that needeth not to be ashamed, rightly dividing the word of truth.*

DEVELOPING BIBLICAL PRINCIPLES FOR LIFE

Many people desire to please God in their lives but wonder how a book full of events from long ago can have any relevance for them today. God has a plan to answer that question. All believers can learn to use the Bible to make decisions about their lives and times even though they are reading a book finished before the end of the first century.

- The first thing to remember is the Bible is no ordinary book. Authored by God using numerous human instruments over many generations to write the words, the Bible is inspired ("God-breathed") by God. The Bible is true, accurate, and authored by God Himself. As such, we can trust its statues, judgments, commandments, and precepts.

- The next key to remember is all believers are illuminated by the Holy Spirit for an understanding of the Word of God. We are indwelt by Him from the moment of salvation and accountable to Him as stewards. Believers, even young believers, receive supernatural help from the Holy Spirit to understand God's written, supernatural book—the Holy Scriptures we call the Bible. Therefore, we should not think Bible study and application is beyond the ability of ordinary believers and just for church leadership and Bible scholars.

- Third, remember Bible study is not through osmosis. You cannot lay down at night with the Bible under your pillow and wake up in the morning knowing more than you did when you went to sleep. Effort is required for Bible study!

Much of Scripture is in the form of narratives—true stories of events and biographies of people. Even many things the Lord Jesus spoke was in the form of parables. The epistles of the New Testament are different, giving some direct commands and doctrines, as is also found in the Old Testament books with the Ten Commandments. Therefore, one of the first things to learn is discerning the difference between **direct precepts** (often phrased as commands) and **derived principles** (must be obtained from a source or origin) from narratives and other passages, which are as inspired as the direct precepts. I believe God did this so each new generation could draw principles from the Word relevant to them in their time and culture.

BIBLE COMMANDS

Bible commands (direct precepts) are passages containing an explicit command from God to His people. They are worded as commands, prohibitions, exhortations, wishes, and permissions. They are the clear do's and don'ts of Scripture and are absolute in terms of their authority. Following are three guidelines for proper interpretation of direct precepts:

— To whom was the precept originally given? Was it originally given in the Old Testament and then given to people living in New Testament times? Was the precept given to people living under the Law, or to all mankind regardless of when they lived? A good rule is to ask, "Has this command been repeated in the New Testament?" This would apply to the Jewish ceremonial laws and others like the Sabbath-day commands. Since they were not repeated in the New Testament, they would not apply. On the other hand, prohibitions against stealing, fornication, greed, murder, and other sins are repeated and thus judged as being applicable to all mankind living in any country, time, or culture.

— What indicates it should be considered normal and appropriate for believers living today and not something only for the culture of the time it was written, such as mourning in sackcloth and ashes, which was a Jewish culture grieving tradition?

— Does it have any contextual, cultural, grammatical, and/or historical meanings affecting its current usage?

DERIVED PRINCIPLES

Derived principles are truths implicitly drawn from narratives, examples, parables, or themed sections of the Word relating to a specific situation from that time and can also be applied to similar situations today.

To be valid, principles must be derived directly from the text without stretching the point, must be affirmed elsewhere in Scripture (Old Testament principle supported by New Testament teaching), and must be consistent with all of the Bible. Scripture, properly interpreted, never contradicts itself; a principle would never contradict a direct precept, nor would two properly derived principles contradict each other.

Principles must be derived by making sure you are studying the Bible correctly—considering the context, the historical setting, the grammatical interpretation, and remembering not to let your own ideas and predispositions alter the intent of Scripture.

It is important to avoid two major dangers in relation to making the Bible come alive and be relevant to you today. The first is the belief interpretation is enough without any application. This is studying the Bible as an academic exercise and teaching it without any persuasive element involved. Stopping at that point does little to challenge you to change the way you live based on God's Word.

The second danger is jumping into application lessons and decisions without an accurate interpretation and understanding of the passage. Either of these can lead to the dangerous practice of adding to or subtracting from the Scripture (*Revelation 22:17–18*). Remember the scathing rebuke Jesus brought against the Pharisees in Matthew 15:9, "*But in vain they do worship me, teaching for doctrines the commandments of men.*"

DIFFERENT TIMES

Remember God authored the Bible, and He intended it for multiple audiences. The first audience is those living at the time it was penned. God used different authors through inspiration to record His words and thoughts for the people being addressed. The second audience is the people living after that in different times, cultures, and countries than the people of Bible times. Therefore, the direct commands or precepts of the Bible are relatively few since they apply to all people everywhere in all times. So, you must now in your time and culture rely on derived principles to help you determine what God would have you do about current situations. For example, nothing in Scripture deals with traffic laws or current entertainment options. You must rely on developing principles from the Word to discern God's will and truth in current issues.

In the process of my ministry with young people, I would often be asked questions about movies, smoking, dancing, and other such subjects dealing with current issues and temptations of life. It is interesting to look back at some of those questions today and note the issue is no longer relevant or debatable as to whether the activity is right or wrong. Some of the issues are considered all right today, and some are not, but the issue has been settled in most believers' minds and biblical understanding. I believe God chose to write the Bible in such a way that with the Holy Spirit's help, proper Bible interpretation, and diligent study, each generation can discern from Scripture how to live for God in the present evil world (*Galatians 1:3–5*).

Because of all those questions, I spent some time and effort to develop a list of principles I shared with my young people when they asked the question about right or wrong issues. I asked them to measure the issue they were wrestling with by this yard stick of ten principles and to consider each one of them in relation to their dilemma. With the use of the ten principles, they could prove whether the activity was good and thus something they could continue doing, or if it was something from which they should abstain.

> 1 Thessalonians 5:21–22—*Prove all things; hold fast that which is good. Abstain from all appearance of evil* (all forms of evil seen).

EXAMPLES OF BIBLICAL PRINCIPLES FOR LIFE

Apply the following principles (*1 Thessalonians 5:21–22*) by proving or testing activities, seeking God's opinion. When activities are neither specifically endorsed nor condemned in the Bible, you may question whether you should participate or not. The question of your participation needs to be answered by the careful interpretation and honest application of such biblical principles. As you consider each of these principles, read all the Bible verses listed for each principle as part of this exercise; make sure you see the principle in each of the passages.

1. Does it cause someone else to sin—stumbling-block principle, the law of love (*Romans 14; 1 Corinthians 8; 1 Corinthians 10:23–33*)?

2. Lay aside not only sins, but every weight which keeps you from being the best possible Christian (*Hebrews 12:1*).

3. Make no provision for the flesh (*Romans 13:14; Galatians 5:16–22*).

4. If it is doubtful, it is dirty (*Romans 14:23; James 4:17*).

5. A Christian should be separate from the world (*2 Corinthians 6:14–7:1; Romans 12:2; 1 John 2:15–17*).

6. Does it glorify God (*1 Corinthians 10:31*)?

7. Would Jesus Christ have done it (*1 Peter 2:21*)?

8. Would you be ashamed if Jesus Christ came and found you doing it (*1 John 2:28*)?

9. Can you feel free to do it when you remember God, the Holy Spirit, dwells within you (*1 Corinthians 6:19*)?

10. Is it fitting conduct for a child of God (*Colossians 1:10; 2 Timothy 2:21–22*)?

In closing, take note it only takes the violation of one principle to determine if a particular life issue in front of you is right or wrong. Violating any one properly derived principle is going against God's revealed truth. Do this exercise carefully, honestly, and wisely.

CHAPTER TEN

Dissolving Doubts by Biblical Principle

If it is doubtful, it is sinful.

Born-again believers can easily determine without direct Bible commands a good number of the choices before them are good choices, and the Lord would be pleased with their participation in them. Conversely, believers can, even with a very minimal knowledge of the Word of God, identify many of life's choices as being wrong for them and thus being sin in God's eyes.

This chapter is not concerned with either of these easily determined lists. Rather, it focuses your attention on everything in between those two lists. The items on this third list are the doubtful things or "issues of life." Concerning these areas, the Bible gives no direct commands. What do you do with this list? How can you discern whether the items on your doubtful list are right or wrong? To illustrate this challenge, look at the "Dissolving Doubts" chart on Study Guide One (page 86). Note the three lists, one titled "Acceptable Things for Me," another labeled "Wrong Things for Me," and between those two columns a third column titled "My Doubtful List." Start with things you cannot at this time prove from the Word of God to be right or wrong. Those doubtful things go in the "My Doubtful List." The exercise's goal is finding biblical proof for knowing to which column the items on "My Doubtful List" should be moved.

The need for this topic is brought about by a very clear verse in Romans. The Apostle Paul was addressing the different opinions of believers concerning the eating of meat available for purchase because the animal had been sacrificed to idols in a pagan, religious ceremony. Those saved out of that false religion thought it would be a sin for them to eat the meat, but other believers knew by faith false gods were not real; therefore, they thought they could eat the meat without sin. Besides, it was cheaper to buy that meat than the meat supplied by farmers in the market place. In the concluding verse of the passage, Paul laid out a clear principle by which those believers in between those two extremes could govern their choices and lives. Paul wrote if someone could not make a decision by faith that their position was right or wrong, then it remained "doubtful," and if it remained doubtful, then God said it was sin.

> Romans 14:23—*And he that doubteth is damned if he eat, because he eateth not of faith: for whatsoever is not of faith is sin.*

Since some doubtful items in life could clearly be acceptable for believers, it is important you develop a method by which you can discern by faith which of the items on the doubtful list should be moved, and to which column they should be moved to.

> 1 Thessalonians 5:21–22—*Prove all things; hold fast that which is good. Abstain from all appearance of evil.*

These two verses command you to be discerning by proving or testing doubtful things so you can discern whether they are good or evil. The phrase "appearance of evil" does not mean "don't do things that look evil";

rather, it means "all kinds of evil seen." This passage is a clear command to you to test doubtful things and come to a biblical conclusion, holding onto the good and abstaining from the evil and the doubtful.

TO BE DISCERNING … OUR DUTY

To follow the teachings of Scripture and be discerning, you must label anything doubtful as sin until by faith you can label it as good. Your responsibility is to test (prove) doubtful things by the truth of the Word of God and exercise biblical discernment so you can label doubtful things as either good or evil.

THE STUDY GUIDES

The following two study guides are helpful as you endeavor to learn and develop discernment. They will help you decide if your doubtful list items can be moved to either the list of good things in which you can participate or the list of things in which you should abstain.

As you begin with the first study guide, remember this is a process to help you make discerning decisions. It may seem like a long process at first, but the more you use it, the faster you will be able to go through the process. Be sure you have satisfied the previously explained prerequisites for discernment in chapter four and have also considered and satisfied the guidelines from the chapter on "Recipe for Discernment."

DIRECTIONS FOR STUDY GUIDE ONE: DISSOLVING DOUBTS

NOTE: Study Guides One and Two are designed to do concurrently with each study guide being helpful in finishing the other.

There are blank worksheets of the two study guides in the appendix for you to copy and write on as you do the exercises.

1. Make sure you understand both *1 Thessalonians 5:21–22* and *Romans 14:23*.

2. List your uncertainties of life's issues in the "My Doubtful List" column.

3. For each issue you are uncertain as to whether it is good or evil, go through each of the ten biblical principles for the issues of life listed in the previous chapter. Consider how each principle might affect or shed light on the issue you are considering from your doubtful list. The list may include questions related to choices concerning clothing and dress, music, entertainment, use of certain words, anger, Sunday activities, boy-girl relationships before marriage, etc.

4. As you come to conclusions on the doubtful issues, cross them off the doubtful list and move them to either the acceptable or wrong column. Your discerned decisions need to come as a result of your prayerful study of God's Word and the application of rightfully-formed principles derived from the Scripture. Document the verses you used and how you came to your conclusions. For future reference, you can review as needed and answer the inevitable question of *why* you came to that conclusion (*1 Peter 3:15*).

5. Occasionally you may need to delay a decision until after you have sought out advice from your spiritual mentors or church leadership, especially if you need some input concerning accurate Bible interpretation.

6. At the end of the worksheet exercise, which may take some time, all items on your doubtful list should be moved to one side or the other; however, you must be truthful in this matter. If the issue is still an area of doubt for you, then the Scripture, based on *Romans 14:22–23*, is clear. You must make your final deci-

sion based on the passage of Scripture from Principle #4: "If it is doubtful, it is dirty."

7. Start the process by listing in the center column two different kinds of issues:

   a. Issues you are unsure of or have the least little bit of doubt concerning whether they are right or wrong.

   b. Issues that you might be asked why you believe them to be right or wrong. The process of going through this exercise will help you give an answer to those questions.

Study Guide One

DISSOLVING DOUBTS

Acceptable Things for Me	My Doubtful List	Unacceptable Things for Me

DIRECTIONS FOR STUDY GUIDE TWO: GROWTH—MOVING FROM DOUBTFUL BOX TO BY FAITH BOX

This study guide is to help you fill out Study Guide Two. Choose an issue on your doubtful column from Study Guide One and write it in the upper box titled "Doubtful Box." Go through the directions in the study guide and write your conclusions based on your biblically-based and prayerful discernment in the lower box titled "By Faith Box." At the end of this exercise, you will by faith move your doubtful life issue to either the "Acceptable Things for Me" or "Unacceptable Things for Me" on Study Guide One.

Now comes the meat of this worksheet. Record in the right column how your biblically-discerned decision necessitates changes in your life. This is called application of truth. Record in the left column the verses and passages on which you based your discernment decision. You should record how you came to this conclusion on this worksheet or in your journal for future reference.

This process takes some time to work through and requires effort and self-discipline to finish for each area of doubt. It is the essence of what the phrase "instruction (training) in righteousness" means in *2 Timothy 3:16*. The promise of achieving discernment (found in verse 17) will not be fulfilled without such disciplined training in the Word. Do not wait until the issue is in your face. Look ahead, settle the issues of potential doubt before they have opportunity to become raging temptations pulling incessantly at your heart and will.

> 2 Timothy 3:16–17—*All scripture is given by inspiration of God, and is profitable for doctrine, for reproof, for correction, for* **instruction in righteousness***: That the man of God may be perfect, thoroughly furnished unto all good works.*

Remember, one of our goals is to eventually arrive at the teaching level of Bible study and discernment. Going through this process equips you to share the reasoning of your conclusions and applications—a necessary step in becoming a teacher of the next generation of question askers.

Study Guide Two

GROWTH

Moving from Doubt to Faith

Doubtful Box

```
┌─────────────────────────────────────────────────────┐
│                                                       │
│                                                       │
└─────────────────────────────────────────────────────┘
```

Bible Principles Considered   Bible Applications and Conclusions

```
┌────────────────────────┐    ┌────────────────────────┐
│                        │    │                        │
├────────────────────────┤    ├────────────────────────┤
│                        │    │                        │
├────────────────────────┤    ├────────────────────────┤
│                        │    │                        │
├────────────────────────┤    ├────────────────────────┤
│                        │    │                        │
├────────────────────────┤    ├────────────────────────┤
│                        │    │                        │
├────────────────────────┤    ├────────────────────────┤
│                        │    │                        │
├────────────────────────┤    ├────────────────────────┤
│                        │    │                        │
├────────────────────────┤    ├────────────────────────┤
│                        │    │                        │
├────────────────────────┤    ├────────────────────────┤
│                        │    │                        │
├────────────────────────┤    ├────────────────────────┤
│                        │    │                        │
├────────────────────────┤    ├────────────────────────┤
│                        │    │                        │
├────────────────────────┤    ├────────────────────────┤
│                        │    │                        │
└────────────────────────┘    └────────────────────────┘
```

```
┌─────────────────────────────────────────────────────┐
│                                                       │
│                                                       │
└─────────────────────────────────────────────────────┘
```

By Faith Box

1 Thessalonians 5:21–22—Prove all things; hold fast that which is good.

CHAPTER ELEVEN

How to Formulate Bible Principles for Life Choices

He who really wants to do something finds a way; he who doesn't finds an excuse.

IS MY HEART PREPARED?

When considering what God desires of you in any given situation where you are uncertain about how to proceed, you may find God's direct precepts or commands do not address every choice you face. Likewise, the ten general principles referred to in the previous two chapters will not fit all the specific issues you may face. Therefore, you must learn how to derive principles from your own personal study and meditation upon the Word. As you do that, you learn the skill of discernment. In *Ezra 7:10*, the Bible says Ezra had prepared his heart to "seek the law of the Lord." He had decided in his heart to a yielded receiving of the Bible as his life authority. He chose to study the Word, not for deciding whether it fit his views and desires, but solely for obeying it. This ought to be your heart's motive as you make daily and long-term decisions.

> 1 Thessalonians 2:13—*For this cause also thank we God without ceasing, because, when ye received the word of God which ye heard of us, ye received it not as the word of men, but as it is in truth, the word of God, which effectually worketh also in you that believe.*

> 2 Timothy 2:15—*Study to shew thyself approved unto God, a workman that needeth not to be ashamed, rightly dividing the word of truth.*

What choice should I make? Which way should I choose to go? What should I do now? How should I handle this situation? Should I change what I am doing, and if so, why? All believers concerned about pleasing God will be asking these questions. It is **not if** these questions will come to mind—they will. The question is—**when will they come**? They often come when the issue is directly in front of you, and an answer needs to be forthcoming. You should be careful about making pressurized decisions. The pressure may be on, but you must remember one of the devil's sneaky tactics is to pressure you with your peers' opinions or the need to answer immediately. If you fall for his strategy, you will be tempted to act without God's input in your life (*2 Corinthians 2:11*). The Lord seldom asks for immediate responses; rather, God's Word admonishes you to consider, meditate, think, and remember when He presents you with a choice of living His way or your own way. God wants you to use the mind He gave you to think through your choices in light of His Word, consider what He has done for you already, meditate upon His Word, and decide with eternity's values in your considerations.

BEWARE OF THE CHALLENGES When Formulating Life Principles

The challenge of the principle's source

If you develop a principle not based on the right authority, it can lead to wrong conclusions. It is easy to let your own opinion infect a principle so some of man's thinking is mixed in with God's thoughts. Anytime you hear the words, "Well, it is my opinion that…," it should raise a red flag in your thinking. You should also beware of allowing the thoughts and opinions of unbelievers, regardless of how logical they may sound, infect your thinking.

> Colossians 2:8—*Beware lest any man spoil you through philosophy and vain deceit, after the tradition of men, after the rudiments of the world, and not after Christ.*

The challenge of keying in on a single principle

Keying in on a single principle can create an overreaction in your thoughts, overruling other principles and sometimes even Bible commands. This leads to an imbalance in deciding on life issues, so you must make sure your principles do not contradict Scripture in either precept or practice. Good principles never do.

The challenge of failure to follow through properly

Good follow-through requires more than just Bible study; it requires application and action. After you do the work of proper Bible study and arrive at an accurate interpretation of the Word, good follow-through requires you not only to formulate biblical principles but also use them to make life-issue decisions. You must not quit before finishing the entire process of principle formation and use.

The challenge of selective application of a solid Bible principle

Weighing the evidence incorrectly because of a personally desired outcome leads to situation ethics, inconsistent behavior, and rationalizing (*Proverbs 11:1–2*).

The challenge of never formulating Bible principles by which to live
If you settle for being a babe in Christ, stuck with a milk diet for life, you will live a spiritually mediocre life and come up short at the Judgment Seat of Christ (*1 Corinthians 3:11–15*). Moreover, the real tragedy is not only will you pay an eternal price, but the next generation you should be teaching will as well.

PRINCIPLE—DEFINING THE TERM

What does the word *principle* mean?

The 1828 Webster's Dictionary Definition[1]:
Principle = Ground; foundation; that which supports an assertion, an action, or a series of actions or of reasoning.

Dictionary App Definition[2]:
Principle = An expression of a fundamental or primary truth from which others are derived, a fundamental doctrine or tenet

---

Our Definition of *Principle*
An **expression of a foundational biblical truth one can rely upon** *to discern good from evil, truth from error; to make right decisions, determine conduct, and distinguish God's will and way from all others.*

Five Characteristics of a Biblical Principle

1. Principles are based on the truth of the Bible and are changeless (*1 Peter 1:25*).

2. Principles do not change with the time or culture in which one lives (*1 Peter 1:23–25*).

3. Principles do not conflict with other rightly-formed principles (*Psalm 19:7–11*).

4. Principles do not have double standards; they apply to all believers (*Romans 10:12*).

5. Principles are valuable when they result in an honest, consistent application to life's issues (*Romans 12:2*).

LAY A BIBLICAL FOUNDATION

- *Ephesians 5:26* says, "That he might sanctify and cleanse it with the washing of water by the word."

- Note the sanctification and cleansing of your mind is brought about by God's Word; therefore, you need to be in the Word, allowing it to wash out the world's things and replace them with God's things.

- *Colossians 3:8–17* and *Ephesians 4:22–24* are parallel passages of Scripture admonishing believers to put off the old man and put on the new man. In other words, stop acting like the unsaved and start acting like a saved person should behave. Notice in both passages a change in thinking based on the truth of God's Word is necessary for change to take place. *Colossians 3:10* says the new man "is renewed in knowledge after the image of him that created him," and *Ephesians 4:23* says, "And be renewed in the spirit of your mind."

- *2 Timothy 3:16* instructs you in the process involved in using the infallible Word of God in a profitable (helpful and serviceable) way.

  All scripture is given by inspiration of God, and is profitable for doctrine, for reproof, for correction, for instruction in righteousness.

The previous passages show the necessity of changing your thinking in order to grow in spiritual maturity; God's Word is necessary in doing that. You need to follow the Bible formula of learning the doctrine, allowing it to reprove your heart, following its direction to correct what you are doing, and applying determined self-discipline in the follow-through toward a righteous lifestyle. After you understand the foundation for discerning principle development requires you to allow and aid the Word in cleaning up your thinking patterns, you must follow the biblical process of change. You can then move on to the process of formulating principles of life.

BUILD ON THE FOUNDATION

You should start with an issue to solve, a difference to settle, or a need for an answer to give. Write the life issue you are seeking to find an answer for on your Principle for Life worksheet. Because the solving of life issues is most likely a personal issue about which you desire discernment and wisdom, the following questions will take on a personal nature as God's Word works in your heart.

Recognize the challenges when formulating life's principles listed on the previous pages and prayerfully ask for God's help in understanding Scripture and avoiding the challenges as you go through this exercise. Start with the truth of God's Word. Find a passage or several passages of Scripture speaking to the area of life you wish to address. Record the Scripture references on the Principle for Life worksheet. Read the passages you have chosen several times. Think through the context and the basic truths being taught in the passages.

FOLLOW THE FOUR-STEP BUILDING PROCESS OF DEVELOPING BIBLICAL DISCERNMENT based on the truth taught in 2 Timothy 3:16–17.

> All scripture is given by inspiration of God, and is profitable for **doctrine**, for **reproof**, for **correction**, for **instruction** in righteousness: That the man of God may be perfect, thoroughly furnished unto all good works.

> Note: There is a Principle for Life worksheet to fill out as you go on page 101 and a reproducible worksheet in the appendix on page 115.

1. **Step One—Doctrine**

   a. Doctrine means teaching or instruction from the Bible.

   b. Figure out what the Scripture passage is teaching.

   c. What does it say? Study it out. This is a deep study process—not just reading over the passage a few times.

   d. What does it mean? Use proper Bible interpretation rules (see appendix for suggested books for help). Write your conclusions about what the basic teaching of the passage means on the Principle for Life worksheet.

   e. Be sure you do not add to or subtract from the Bible (*Proverbs 30:5–6*).

   f. Ask God for His help from the Holy Spirit to illuminate your mind and heart on what this passage means.

2. **Step Two—Reproof**

   a. Reproof is the Word of God showing you your sin (*Hebrews 4:12–13*).

   b. The Holy Spirit will help here as He convicts you of your sin (*John 16:8*) and coming short of the glory of God (*Romans 3:23*).

   c. What do you need to repent of before continuing (*1 John 1:9*)?

   d. Consider at this juncture your motivations since *James 4:1–4* tells you God does not answer your prayers when offered up with the wrong motivations.

   e. The Word also shows you some behaviors that need to be put off (*Colossians 3:5–9; Ephesians 4:22, 25–31*).

   f. Record on the Principle for Life worksheet any issues you need to solve with the development of this principle.

3. **Step Three—Correction**

   a. God's Word also tells you how to do it right. You must appreciate the balance of His Word in not only telling you what you are doing wrong (reproof) but also telling you how to do it right (correction).

   b. Based on the correction of the Word, what should you be willing to do?

   c. Record the results of this correction on the *Principle of Life* worksheet. This exercise indicates what you have learned from studying these passages.

   d. At this point take some time to meditate upon how these corrections fit with your overall life goals, mission, and your willingness to yield to the Lord.

   e. Share the results of some of these meditations, considerations, and conclusions with others as it is appropriate to do so.

   f. Be sure to record them in your journal.

4. **Step Four—Instruction** (discipline) **in Righteousness** (righteous living)

a. "Instruction" (Greek word *paideia*) primarily means disciplined training in how to live righteously in life. As a coach would verbally instruct, physically instruct, and require a disciplined approach to developing athletic skills, so will the Word of God work to develop your spiritual life.

b. This process takes character and endurance to follow through to the desired end. Are you willing to run the race of your life with such discipline? (*1 Corinthians 9:24–27; Hebrews 12:1–3; 2 Timothy 2:5; 4:7*)

c. An accountability journal or partner will help you to follow through with the discipline to finish the race God has for you to run.

d. Record your action goals for applying the principle to your life.

What is the result of this kind of in-depth Bible study?

2 Timothy 3:17—*That the man of God may be perfect, thoroughly furnished unto all good works.*

Consider Questions

Read these three passages of Scripture. Note the key teaching of each of them and record the result.

1. *James 1:21–25*

   Key

   Result

2. *Romans 12:1–2*

   Key

   Result

3. *Luke 6:46–49*

   Key

   Result

Principle for Life Worksheet

I desire to develop a biblically-based principle providing me guidance in discerning what pleases God concerning this life issue:

List the Scripture references you will study to determine this principle.

Identify and write out the proof text for this principle from the list above.

What is the basic teaching or doctrine of these Scripture passages?

Write out the principle derived from these passages.

Personal Application Developed from the Four-Step Process of Biblical Change:

1. How has the reproof of the Word convicted my heart?

2. Has the conviction been dealt with biblically?

3. Is my heart prepared to seek the truth from the Word?

4. How do I need to adjust my thinking in order to develop discernment that pleases God?

5. What changes (corrections) will I endeavor, with God's help, to make by applying this principle to my life? What behaviors do I need to put off and put on?

6. What action goals do I need to apply to put this principle of operation in my life?

7. What is my accountability plan?

---

1   "principle." *WebstersDictionary1828.com*. 2019. Web. 30 April 2019.

2   "principle." *Dictionary.com*. 2019. Web. 30 April 2019.

CHAPTER TWELVE

Exercising Discernment

For every one that useth milk is unskilful in the word of righteousness: for he is a babe. But strong meat belongeth to them that are of full age, even those who by reason of use have their senses exercised to discern both good and evil.
Hebrews 5:13–14

As noted before, one of the key verses in the Bible discussing the development of discernment is *Hebrews 5:14*, pointing out two aspects to learning the skill of discernment. The first aspect is becoming knowledgeable and proficient in the Word of God. Such knowledge results in your being able to understand the deeper things of the Word (strong meat). This leads to your becoming spiritually mature (full age), progressing from being a "babe in Christ" through a consistent and prayerful study of the Word of God, and becoming "full age" in Christ.

The second crucial aspect to developing the skill of discernment involves the exercise and use taught in verse 14b, "…those who by **reason of use** have their senses **exercised** to discern both good and evil." This is not physical exercise but the exercising of your mental muscles.

If you desire to learn discernment so it becomes an automatic response to life issues, use the process described in chapter ten. You also need to develop a plan to grow in your discernment skill by practicing it until you can simply, without much work, discern the difference between good and evil in your daily life. Looking at this verse a little closer, you find it gives a formula for doing just that.

The following words were defined in chapter one, but look how Albert Barnes in his commentary on *Hebrews 5:14* defines these three words or phrases.

Senses

Barnes says, "the word used here means…'the internal sense,' the faculty of perceiving truth;… The meaning is, that by long experience Christians come to be able to understand the more elevated doctrines of Christianity; they see their beauty and value, and they are able carefully and accurately to distinguish them from error."[1]

Exercised

The word *exercised* means to train as an athlete trains and practices to perfect his skills. In the same way a Christian needs to train and practice the skill of discernment; therefore, when your senses are exercised, you are training your senses to be discerning.

Reason of Use

One more qualifier is found in this phrase, *by reason of use*. Barnes again says of this phrase, "The Greek word means 'habit, practice.' The meaning is, that by long use and habit they had arrived to that state in which they could appreciate the more elevated doctrines of Christianity."

---

1   Commentary notes on Hebrews 5:14. Barnes, Albert. *Notes on the Bible*, e-Sword 11.0.6 edition. 2019.

In conclusion, Scripture teaches if you desire to learn the skill of discerning between good and evil for everyday life and use, you need to decide to put some time and effort into it as an athlete working to perfect a skill. Practice, practice, practice … applying Scripture truth to everyday life.

EXAMPLE OF PRACTICING SPIRITUAL DISCERNMENT

The book of Proverbs is a key book in learning to apply God's truth to everyday life. In the first seven verses of the book, it states several times its purpose is to teach the simple (unwise novice) to be wise. Therefore, the more time you spend in Proverbs, the more you see life through God's eyes, apply wisdom gained from God's Word, and use that wisdom in your teaching of others. So this exercise is about learning to discipline yourself to be consistent in the Word in finding principles to live by, and it is also about learning from the book of Proverbs.

Start by reading a chapter of Proverbs every day of the month (31 chapters in Proverbs = one chapter per day, doubling up a few times). Do this consistently for a year or more. As you are reading, discipline yourself to find one general principle for life from what you read every day for the entire year. Record your principles in a journal (at the end of a year you should have over 350 principles recorded). At first, this will seem difficult, but the longer you do it, the easier it gets, and soon you will be seeing principles in other Bible reading as well. Record those too. If you do this consistently, you will be surprised how often what you have read and recorded as Bible principles crop up in your conversation. This helps in discerning God's will and truth in your present-life issues or in someone seeking advice or counsel from you. You will with time and practice become a spiritually mature person who "*by reason of use have their senses exercised to discern both good and evil.*"

THE ROLE OF FAITH IN DISCERNMENT

You have no reason for using Scripture for discerning good from evil if you have no faith in their absolute truth and accept them as the very words of God. You must have an absolute confidence in the veracity and truth of God's Word because it is the measuring stick you use to evaluate every idea, tradition, philosophy, conclusion, teaching, and opinion of man. If they do not measure up to the standard of truth in His Word, reject them. If you waver in your faith, you will also waver in your determination to live by faith as a spiritually mature believer, discerning truth from error.

How Do You Build Your Faith?

- **Study the Word.**
  Romans 10:17—*So then faith cometh by hearing, and hearing by the word of God.*

- **Ask for faith in prayer.**
  Mark 9:24—*And straightway the father of the child cried and said with tears, Lord, I believe; help thou mine unbelief.*

- **Live by faith.**
  2 Corinthians 5:7—*For we walk by faith, not by sight.*

Just start acting and making decisions based on what the Word says, and your faith will grow.

Faith is the **belief** in the unseen things talked of in the Bible and **acting** upon their reality.

Do not quit learning and developing your spiritually mature ability to discern God's will and way from all others. Since the Bible is authored by an infinite, all-knowing God, you will never in your lifetime fathom its true depths. With the Holy Spirit's help, the Word of God will keep opening and expanding new vistas of understanding and insight into the nature of your wonderful Triune God—the Father, Son, and Holy Spirit.

Appendix

Chapter Seven Answers, pages 62–63

When for a **TIME**
You ought to be **TEACHERS**
But you are **BABES**

Babes in Christ/Teachers chart

BABES IN CHRIST (*no particular order, but they contrast with Teacher chart by number*)

1. D*ull of hearing = not a learner*
2. *Needs teaching even the simple things of the Word*
3. *Dull = sluggish, slothful when it comes to study of the Word*
4. *Babes = spiritually immature*
5. *Milk (liquid diet as a baby), no teeth*
6. *You have need*
7. *You need to start by learning*
8. *Unskillful in the Word*

9. *No use or application of Scripture for life issues*
10. *Never knows why they do what they do*
11. *Unable to use the Bible as a tool to figure out what to do in order to please God*
12. *Has a lazy mind cluttered with thorns and weeds (Matthew 13:22)*

TEACHERS

1. *Senses exercised*
2. *Knows elementary doctrine*
3. *Energetic in learning*
4. *Full age = spiritually mature*
5. *Meat (solid food) of the Scripture*
6. *Ye ought to be (should already be) spiritually mature*
7. *Ye ought to be teachers of others*
8. *Senses exercised = trained and used to make distinctions*
9. *By reason of use = doing it regularly*
10. *Able to discern*
11. *Able to distinguish between good and evil*
12. *Exercised mind = using it to apply truth to situations of life*

RESOURCES

Notes on the Whole Bible by Albert Barnes
Bible Explorer's Guide by John Phillips
Dangerous Parenting Detours by Walt Brock
Strong's Exhaustive Concordance to the Bible by James Strong
www.e-sword.net

SAMPLE JOURNAL PAGE

DAILY BIBLE JOURNAL   DATE _____

THANK YOU FOR
1.
2.
3.

BIBLE READING NOTES

FORGIVE ME FOR   TODAY I'M PRAYING FOR

MY VERSE FOR TODAY

DISCERNMENT NOTES & THOUGHTS

DISSOLVING DOUBTS

Acceptable Things for Me	My Doubtful List	Unacceptable Things for Me

GROWTH

Moving from Doubt to Faith

Doubtful Box

```
┌─────────────────────────────────────────────┐
│                                               │
└─────────────────────────────────────────────┘
```

Bible Principles Considered	Bible Applications and Conclusions

```
┌─────────────────────────────────────────────┐
│                                               │
└─────────────────────────────────────────────┘
```

By Faith Box

1 Thessalonians 5:21–22—Prove all things; hold fast that which is good.

Principle for Life Worksheet

I desire to develop a biblically-based principle providing me guidance in discerning what pleases God concerning this life issue:

List the Scripture references you will study to determine this principle.

Identify and write out the proof text for this principle from the list above.

What is the basic teaching or doctrine of these Scripture passages?

Write out the principle derived from these passages.

Western Adventure in Christian Camping

A place to get away and consider
A place of encouragement in your Christian walk
An opportunity of Christian fellowship
Camps and retreats available for all ages

www.ironwoodcamp.org

For more resources, visit our online bookstore
www.ShopIronwood.org
49191 Cherokee Road
Newberry Springs, CA 92365
Phone: 760.257.3503
info@ironwood.org

Made in United States
Orlando, FL
22 October 2023

38131411R00065